Integrity-Based Communications

Using Truth To Build High-Trust Relationships

All the best ~
Shelley Bauer

6-23-15

Integrity-Based Communications

Using Truth To Build High-Trust Relationships

Shelley Page Baur

For John,

whose unconditional love inspires me to be

my personal best.

Table of Contents

Acknowledgements

Before Integrity-Based Communications was a book, it was a series of keynote speeches with companion seminars. By 1992, I was first introduced to Life Design Seminars' "Five Points of Personal Power," which evolved into the six behaviors of Integrity-Based Communications. Thank you, Paul, Michelle and Susan for changing my life!

I was greatly influenced in keynote development by Juanell Teague, a speakers' coach in Dallas and author of *The Zig Ziglar Difference.*

It was while attending Brian Tracy's *The Phoenix Seminar for Maximum Achievement* that I answered the question, "What would you do if you knew you could not fail?" My answer was: "To write a book that would change people's lives." Ten years later, this book was published. My message is one of communicating with straightforward simplicity, and I thank Brian Tracy for the challenge.

Many people have been encouraging and helpful in the refinement process of this material: John Baur, my husband, who lets me test the behaviors at home daily and encourages me with his unrelenting example of self-discipline; Mandi Stanley, a top-notch presenter whom I admire and respect greatly; Judy Bell, an amazing friend, business colleague and Mastermind partner; and Bonnie Taylor, a leadership coach and teacher who helped me "get out of my own way" and design a higher path. Her joy is contagious, and I can't imagine where my life would be without her.

Brenda Younger and Walter Kimbrough are two very special colleagues who helped me challenge and refine this theory as seminar curriculum collaborators, both of whom lead with their hearts and their heads. Brenda was especially helpful, freely sharing her library and research as I moved ahead on this project. Fellow Toastmasters and seminar co-presenters Mark Cardona and David Stolzle became accountability partners as all three of us tackled our "first book" projects simultaneously. It has been fun and rewarding, both personally and professionally.

Karen Smith has shared my journey into integrity, personally and professionally, and ably wore many hats in preparing the first edition of this book. For all this and more, many thanks, Karen.

Ed Champagne has been one of my most significant career mentors, as an extraordinary people-builder, generous provider of resources, and encourager of my lifelong learning pursuits. From our shared experience with *The Phoenix Seminar* to Development Dimensions International (DDI) to customized curricula, I am deeply indebted to Ed for his attitude of abundance and his impeccable ethics. He is a true servant leader.

Bradley Harris has been a champion of this project,

pushing me to deeper insights, broader insights, higher reaches. It helps me to have accountability partners who are also good friends.

Finally, I thank my loving family, especially my husband John Baur and Marion Page, my mother, who both endured my growth pains during the "book birthing" process. I am also very grateful to the friends who contributed relevant stories and the clients who continually testify that Integrity-Based Communications—using truth to build high-trust relationships—actually works, in every aspect of life. Thank you for staying connected and for affirming that our truth does indeed set us free!

Introduction
Integrity-Based Communications

Dealing in truth...
To give real service you must add something which cannot be
bought or measured with money, and that is
sincerity and integrity.

– Donald A. Adams

What is integrity? Depending on the dictionary you consult, you will find such words as "moral uprightness, sincerity, wholeness, being complete." "Honesty" is a close, though not perfect, synonym. Today my definition of personal integrity is this: integrating ways of thinking, communicating and behaving that consistently reflect the highest standards of ethical behavior; bringing together of necessary parts to make a whole.

Ultimately, the goal is to improve relationships. As Brian Tracy puts it, "Integrity is the quality that guarantees all the other values."

Integrity-Based Communications (IBC) is a method that can be used to positively affect success through six behaviors, used consistently:

1. Tell your truth quicker, faster.
2. Ask for what you want.
3. Ask questions to discover others' motivators.
4. Pay attention!

5. Keep your agreements.

6. Give and receive accountability.

IBC also rests on a solid understanding of how we humans often *do* communicate, and an understanding of what affects the quality of our communication. Here, too, stand six important ideas. Six *axioms*, we call them, because they are descriptions of six facts, six factors that will determine how well (or, sometimes, badly) we communicate. The six axioms are:

1. All truth is perceptual, filtered, interpreted.

2. We want what we want, but sometimes we aren't clear about it.

3. We presume more than we ask.

4. Most of us speak sooner than listen, pay attention less well than we think we do.

5. Most of us make and keep agreements less well than we believe we do.

6. We are all afraid of accountability.

These axioms are observations about how communication often actually operates. The whole point of this book is that our communication doesn't have to suffer from the problems these six axioms present. But to avoid these problems, we must first see them, grasp them, own them. That's part of learning and mastering the IBC process. You'll read more about these axioms as we look at the six IBC behaviors.

IBC is a relationship improvement process that emphasizes values, which respect and honor all people. Empathetic listening, speaking and behavior really can reduce stress and create a more balanced environment, transforming people and relationships into the best they can be.

In numerous business surveys, "honesty" ranks as the leadership trait most admired by employees – 87% is the statistic used most consistently by such respected leadership authors as James M. Kouzes and Barry Z. Posner [1].

In the aftermath of Enron, Arthur Andersen, WorldCom, Tyco…housing and financial collapse…and other headline scandals uncovered in the new millennium, the public pendulum has swung back to a clear craving for ethics and "squeaky-clean" practices. In business, politics and religion, the mandate is clear – we want the truth!

On a personal level, healthy relationships are based on honesty, loyalty and commitment. How many people want to marry someone who promises to be "99%" committed? Only when we are willing to share our truth – spoken with care and respect—with partners, colleagues and friends, can we relate deeply and authentically. This book explores how to do so.

To quote the wisdom of Warren Buffet...

In looking for people to hire, look for three qualities: integrity, intelligence, and energy. If you don't have the first, the other two will kill you.

And this...

It takes ten years to build a reputation, and five minutes to kill it. If you think about that you'll do things differently.

chapter 1

Tell Your Truth Quicker, Faster

Learning your truth…
> *In order to become the person you wish*
> *to become, you must first think, walk, talk and act*
> *as if you already are that person.*

— Earl Nightengale

First Axiom: Some truth about truth. We often speak about "the" truth, as if it were singular, as if it were purely objective, standing apart, as if we ourselves had nothing to do with what truth is. But truth doesn't seem to work that way. Now is that to say there is no objective truth, to pronounce casually that "It's all relative"? Not at all. But what we will say is that, in our looking for truth, dealing with truth, we too often forget that perception gets in the way.

Think about an argument between two friends or family members …"But you said…"…"I said no such thing!"…"Yes, you did. You sat right there and told me…" You see where this is going—nowhere, but fast. Each is determined that *his* memory, what *she* believes, is right. Uniquely right. This argument isn't going to get resolved until someone says, "Well, what I *heard* you say was…"

What's the difference? So long as one person

continues to splutter, "But you said...," that person is talking about *absolute* truth. But as soon as she switches to "Well, what I *heard* you say was..." something significant has happened. First, this person has acknowledged that the truth she claims is what she *heard*, is the truth *as shaped by her own understanding and perception.* Second, she's opened the door to the other person's making a similar admission. And that, in turn, opens the door to a calmer talk, authentic talk, and a possible resolution.

Right there you have it—that first of our six axioms:
All truth is perceptual, filtered, interpreted.

Your truth, not "the" truth. In years past, I would have said, "Tell the truth," crediting the "Five Points of Personal Power" that I learned in *Life Design Seminars.* Since then I've learned that there is usually more than one perspective on the truth—any truth. I can only be responsible for understanding, embracing and living my truth as I understand it, moment by moment. My job is not to impose my truth on anyone. It's only to share it with the willingness to be open-minded in hopes that sharing differing views on "the truth" may broaden the worldview of each participant.

Quicker, faster. Thanks to professional speaking coach Juanell Teague,[2] I use this redundancy intentionally. The quicker I tell my version of the truth, the faster I will get the result I want…which is using my truth to get what I *really* want for myself and others. It is a collaborative process, and it must begin with me.

Using my truth to get what I really want began by first discovering what I *really do* want. For me, there was a time when I believed that "Life is Difficult." Yes, with a capital D. Most of my knowledge came through painful life experiences I didn't want to repeat! I learned what I wanted largely through the process of elimination — what I now call "living by default."

Today, it is my willingness to get clear about what I really do want, to focus only on that, and to clearly articulate "my truth" that helps me attract the desired result into my life and into my relationships. This clarity accelerates my relationships to a deeper, more authentic level and dramatically enhances mutual understanding. It also reduces the stress in my life, because truth-telling means never having to explain (or remember) a lie!

Second Axiom: We want what we want, but sometimes we aren't clear about it. We're individuals. We want different things. We have different motivators. Things motivate us differently — money, for example, highly motivates one person, but motivates another less. Sometimes we aren't as clear as we could be about what we want. Other times, we don't think deeply enough about our wants, and presume either that others understand them, or that "everybody" wants what we do. Sometimes, we aren't even clear in our own minds.

Let me pose some questions and share some examples that bring this theory to life. How many times have you invited someone to share a meal and you couldn't decide where to go? The conversation may go something like: "Where would you like to go?" with the reply, "I don't care—you decide" or "Wherever you want to go." If every suggestion is met with an objection such as "Oh, I just had that yesterday" or "That's too fattening," the frustration level may lead to re-thinking the offer! Better to say, "Anything but spicy" or "Anyplace I can have fresh vegetables" so that *your* truth helps define the choices, avoids frustration and reduces stress levels.

In a business setting, truth-telling is a critical habit that helps us to save time, lower stress, and give others the information they need to make informed decisions. Better to put your truth on the table during the meeting than in the hall or at the water cooler meeting-after-the-meeting. Hindsight may be 20-20, but it sure is costly if your truth, your opinion, your idea wasn't given the benefit of consideration because you didn't speak up!

Here's another thought to consider: Don't just "go along to get along" with people. In the short run, you may be seen as friendly and easy-going, but in the long run, your teammates aren't getting access to that wonderful brain of yours...which could have helped deliver a better solution, faster.

Sometimes truth-telling is as simple as a neutral, non-threatening conversation opener, such as:

- *I need access to your brain for about fifteen minutes.*
- *It's time for a reality check.*
- *This isn't working for me. I need help!*

Rather than using e-mail or the telephone to speak your truth, I recommend setting up an in-person meeting. Making a phone call would be my second choice. I would only use e-mail or text messaging for delivering simple facts, such as a time and place for a meeting, or eliciting a straightforward yes-or-no answer that needs no further explanation. That may sound surprising to readers who have come to rely on these quick, easy modes of communication. According to a study by Albert Mehrabian, however, the relative value of three major components of "effective communication" is as follows:

- 7% words
- 38% tone of voice
- 55% body language. [3]

To put it another way, body language—glaring eyes or back turned, for example—delivers more believability than does one's tone of voice—for example, an apparently sincere *Everything's fine.* Tone of voice—sarcasm, say—counts more than words. Imagine different tones in which a person might deliver a line such as *I have nothing to do but wait for you.*

The numerical values given above shouldn't be read strictly, of course. The point is: When words, voice tone, and body language aren't in synch, we give mixed messages. And that, by itself, is a violation of integrity in communication.

To convey your truth more completely and effectively, be consistent in your communicating. Give your communication partner(s) the benefit of your *whole* self—not just your words, but your non-verbal cues as well.

Maintain or enhance self-esteem.[4] Borrowed from the "Key Principles" of Pittsburgh-based Development Dimensions International, Inc. (DDI), this is a reminder that the goal in any communication includes showing respect and nurturing relationships. In other words, don't tell the truth unkindly and say, "Well, it's the truth!" (as if chopping people off at the kneecaps were acceptable, as long as what we say happens to be factual). Instead, be willing to change the dynamic by saying, gently, "There is a kinder way to speak that truth. Let's try again."

To get what I really want...My favorite "tell my truth quicker, faster" story involves meeting and marrying my husband, John Baur. I had been mentoring a talented young woman studying piano performance at The University of Memphis, Ruska "Rusi" Mchedlishvili. This gifted 19- year-old student had become involved with a young man whom I had stereotyped as a "loser," based on Rusi's description of him. Knowing that a direct indictment of this young man would not result in building the kind of long-term friendship I wanted with Rusi, I used my experience of unsuccessful romantic relationships as an example of having settled for less than I really wanted, with very unhappy consequences. I actually took her through a "values clarification" exercise [5] from the seminar *Living on Purpose: Tools for Building the Life You* Really *Want*,[6] and explained why certain values (like spirituality, honesty, commitment, and intimacy) were important to me, the meanings I attached to each of those values, and what the associated behaviors looked like.

Though I wasn't emotionally invested in the outcome of Rusi's situation, sharing "my truth" resonated with her truth. She could relate her unhappiness to mine. Ultimately, she did break up with the young man, which left open the space to find and marry her "right man." For me, it was worth being vulnerable and exposing my perceived failure to help my young friend discover her own truth and find true happiness. How many times do we (or people we know) settle for less than we want or deserve? Being honest with *oneself* is the beginning to being honest with others.

By the way, my willingness to talk about what I *really* wanted in my life triggered Rusi's belief that the "perfect man" for me was the handsome, single associate director whom she knew and respected at The University of Memphis. She began a yearlong, underground campaign to get us together! It worked, and we still act like two love-struck teens. Now calling ourselves "Poster Children for Hope"...as in hope for those people who have given up, thinking that they can't have the love they always dreamed of having, or live the life they always wanted. John Baur and I know it is possible. We live it every day.

Don't delay what you intend to deny. Sometimes we just go along to get along with people, afraid that they won't like us if we tell *our* truth, especially where it differs from others' truths. We may say nothing at all, or if being asked to do something we don't want to do, we might say, "Let me get back to you." When I know that my plate is full and that I simply cannot squeeze one more thing into my tightly packed calendar, I've learned that I am far more peaceful if I just go ahead and gently decline the request. I'll say something like, "I'd much rather disappoint you on the front end by saying 'no' now, than disappoint you on the back end because I never should have said 'yes.' I know you understand." Or: "I wish I could, but I'm over-committed as it is." This last example can be used repeatedly, in the same conversation, as they attempt to convince you against your will. Just keep saying, over and over, "I wish I could."

Sometimes I have to get a bit more direct—albeit with

humor—and ask, "What is it you don't understand about the word *no*? Is it the 'N' or the 'O'?"

Lynn McDonald is a dear friend I met through BNI: Business Network International,[7] a structured group that meets weekly to share business referrals. She tells a personal and business story that illustrates the best of telling your truth quicker, faster...

> *My daughter, Vicki, was about to graduate from college with a degree in broadcast engineering when she surprised me by asking, "How can I get an interview with you, Mom?" This was a complete surprise to me because she had worked hard to get her degree. I had never thought about her working with me at my Allstate insurance agency and perhaps someday taking it over.*
>
> *Of course I welcomed my daughter with open arms, and she was a great asset. She had wonderful people skills, and my clients enjoyed her so much. When it came about that I was going to remarry and eventually move to Memphis, Tennessee, it was apparent that she would be in a position to take over ownership of the agency sooner than had been expected.*
>
> *During the three years Vicki worked with me she maintained a part-time position with the Public Broadcasting Service (PBS), a relationship she had*

started in high school and continued through college. Eventually came the time when we needed to discuss transferring ownership. What courage it must have taken for my daughter to tell me, "I don't know if I want to work this hard and someday try to raise a family, too. I don't think I want to be an insurance agent for my career."

Without hesitation I replied, "As a potential future Grandma, I think you are making the right decision." I know Vicki was afraid she might hurt my feelings by turning down my business, but that decision has blessed both our lives. She has gone on to do very well with PBS using the skills she has worked hard to develop. I found another purchaser for my Wisconsin agency, which provided me money to invest in my Memphis agency. And as a caring parent, I am grateful that my daughter was able to tell me the truth about how she felt. There would have been tremendous guilt on my part if I had ever discovered that Vicki had sacrificed her own desires in place of mine. Since then, she has blessed me with two grandsons!

In his newspaper column *More Than Work,*[8] Tim McGuire, one of my all-time favorite writers, clearly articulated the truth-telling bottom line, "We do no one any favors if we obfuscate and hint because we want to be gentle."

In fact, our willingness to *Tell our truth quicker, faster* is both a way of communicating and an intentional way to demonstrate the behavior we want from others. With a shy but coachable friend or colleague, try this prompt: *Tell your truth quicker, faster. It will help me understand where you stand—without having to wonder—and it will save time for both of us.*

In response to an aggressive comment, truthful coaching might involve physically moving away and saying, "Wow! That feels a bit 'in your face' to me. It could be received as a bit overpowering...or even threatening."

Truth telling is the very model of leadership, a model that builds high-trust relationships, no matter where or how you find yourself in a position to set an example for others to follow.

If you tell the truth, you don't have to remember anything.
— Mark Twain

Think About It!

After reading these examples, perhaps you can think of a time when telling your truth more quickly might have resulted in a speedier, more positive resolution. Jot down the circumstances and date of today's awareness. If you note today's date, this time reference can become a powerful reminder of the progress you are making, using truth telling to get what you *really* want.

Today's date: —————————————————————————

Situation: —————————————————————————

—————————————————————————————————

Using my truth for the desired outcome:

—————————————————————————————————

—————————————————————————————————

—————————————————————————————————

You'll find more space to think through these and related questions in Chapter 8—Your Thinking Cap.

chapter 2

Ask for What You Want

Simplifying your truth...
Your vision will become clear only when
you can look into your own heart.

— Carl Jung

Earlier in my life, I explored how I was conditioned (either by my parents or others in authority) not to ask for what I wanted. I realized that I was afraid to ask because I was afraid of rejection, that I wouldn't be liked, that people would say "no." Finally, I realized that people could not read my mind, so I had to be willing to take the risk to ask for what I wanted, with straightforward simplicity. If I didn't ask, I probably wouldn't receive, and I was likely to be disappointed by "settling" for less than I really wanted in life and in relationships (since that was what I had been experiencing so far). When I became willing to ask for what I wanted, my success rate improved!

Continuing with my earlier dining example, I know that I have defaulted many times, only to eat others' choices when I failed to give an opinion or establish parameters. That's what I call "living by default" instead of "living on purpose," being intentional. Who wants someone else's leftovers? Choose to participate and you'll see how liberating this new habit can be!

Here's what I recommend to people whose habit is to hold back or avoid asking for what they want because they are afraid of rejection...

For a week, every time you get on an elevator or make eye contact with someone on the street, simply smile. Every time you see someone, just smile. It's that simple. You're not making a request, but you are creating a habit of doing something to build a new relationship that is non-threatening. It's generally easy to get comfortable with this new behavior.

The second week, give a sincere compliment to everyone you meet. It can be about anything—an article of clothing the person is wearing, a beautiful smile, displaying a positive attitude—so long as your compliment really is sincere. At the end of this week, you'll be surprised that everyone is so friendly.

The third week, whenever you meet someone new, say to them, "I'm in training. May I give you my business card?" Perhaps to your surprise, complete strangers will be more than willing to accept your card.

By then, you'll have created a new habit of finding people warm, smiling, and receptive. (It takes only 21 days to create a new habit, the "experts" say).

Approaching people will have lost any fear it's held for

you, even when you meet someone who doesn't appear so friendly.

My thought is: "When you see someone without a smile, go ahead and give them one of yours." It costs nothing, contains no calories, and it is fully returnable. The very worst your smile will do is: nothing. And it might well lead to a new friend, a new contact...maybe even new business.

Third Axiom: We presume more than we ask. It *seems* easier to presume —at least, to begin with. You don't have to say anything. Don't have to be assertive. You just...wait. After all, *shouldn't* the waiter know you need more mozzarella? And your friends—*shouldn't* they know you will need their help moving to your new home? We presume others know our needs. Often, too, we presume we know what others need or want.

Asking for referrals. In a business and networking settings such as Business Network International (BNI), here's how this aspect of Integrity-Based Communications (IBC) works, according to a story passed along to me by Lois Bennett, an associate with Coldwell Banker in Sarasota, Florida. When Lois first realized that she had to ask for referrals, she tried it with a friend, who seemed taken aback, says Lois.

"I asked whether I'd offended her," says Lois, and the friend replied, "No, but that didn't sound like you." You see, Lois had never asked for referrals before and didn't know how to ask. That friend went on to give Lois more than $5 million in referral business. Now Lois Bennett adds a P.S. to every letter asking for referrals.

"Givers gain" philosophy.[9] Lois went on to say this:

> On a deeper level, my helping others understand what I want—and why—makes it easier for them to say "yes" to my requests. When I have invested time to find out what is important to other people, I generally discover that they are interested in finding out what is important to me. Practicing this weekly in BNI meetings, I learned that these little exchanges can build new relationships into really treasured friendships. My experience is that people want to do business with, and refer business to, people they know, like and trust.
>
> success I have had in life. Of course, the first healthy relationship I needed to have was with myself, and it was critical to get very, very clear about what was true for me. How else could I articulate my truth with any authenticity? Or know what to ask for?

In Lewis Carroll's classic book *Through the Looking Glass*,[10] Alice comes to an intersection in Wonderland where she must choose which direction to take. When she looks, she notices the smiling Cheshire cat up in the tree. Alice says,

"Oh, please, sir, will you tell me which road to take?" He replies, "Where are you trying to go?" and Alice says, "I don't know." The Cheshire cat smiles and says, "Well, then, any road will get you there."

The lesson? First, we have to know where we are (learn the truth about ourselves) and secondly, we have to know where we want to go, envisioning our desired future. If you do not know where you want to go, take some time to reflect on that now.

> *This above all: To thine own self be true.*
> — William Shakespeare

Think About It!

Think about your primary goal in life.
What do you *really* want? _____

_____

In what way would you like to take charge of your own
future? _____

_____

Now think about some contributory goals...
What is your primary goal in romance? _____

_____

What would you attempt if you knew you could not fail?

_____

Are you aware of anything holding you back from reaching
these goals? Anything you need to change?

_____

_____

Stop for just a moment to think of a time when you
took a risk to ask for what you wanted and the outcome was
better than you had anticipated—as with Lois Bennett.

Can you imagine a time when a parent kept telling a
story about you as a 16-year-old? Does anyone want to be
locked into teenage history? Not knowing how your parent
would react, perhaps you made the request anyway. To your
surprise and delight, the response was, "I had no idea that

story bothered you. Thanks for telling me."

Personally, when I had that exact experience in my early 30's, it was a turning point in the relationship with my mother. When I shared this with her recently, she didn't even remember the incident. For me, it was the day I began relating to her as one adult to another, which has allowed our relationship to grow deeper, richer, and better ever since.

Think about a relationship that could be improved by taking a risk and asking for what you want.

_____

_____

_____

When will you do this? _____

You'll find more space to think through these and related questions in Chapter 8—Your Thinking Cap

chapter **3**

Ask Questions to Discover Others' Motivators

Learning others' truth…

> *Seek first to understand, then to be understood.*
>
> — Stephen Covey

People do things for *their* reasons – not yours. Early in my adult life, I realized that unless I personally held positional power or financial power over others, they might not do what I wanted them to do. What a shock! In fact, people usually do things for *their* reasons, not mine! If I want to develop those elusive win-win outcomes—for all constituents—I must find ways to uncover what each party truly wants in order to work toward that goal ("Begin with the end in mind," as Stephen Covey says in *The Seven Habits of Highly Effective People* [11]).

Psychologists say that we do things for one of two reasons: to gain pleasure or to avoid pain. How many people can still be controlled by a parent's raised eyebrow—even across the room? Or the guilt inducing tone of voice from a friend who wants you to do something (usually for their reasons, not understanding yours)?

My key to successful relationships is discovering what motivates and inspires people to action. To win their support my vision must mesh with their goals, dreams, intent, purpose, and drive. The only way I can discover what's important to others is to ask them with sincere interest and genuine curiosity, helping them flesh out the details so that I learn more about what they do want than what they don't want.

Fourth Axiom: Most of us speak sooner than listen, pay attention less well than we think we do. Do you know someone who "talks too much"? (If you do, first recognize that this may be *your* truth—not theirs!) One thing big talkers often do is answer their own questions: "Where would you like to go for dinner, dear? Because, there's that new Chinese place. And Milano's—you like Milano's. Fleming's—how about a steak at Fleming's? Of course, we could always just see what there is along Winchester..." The answer this speaker is likely to get—presuming a polite partner—is something along the lines of: "Wherever you'd like—you decide."

It's easy to pick on domestic partnerships for bad examples. But no less often do they happen at the office, within volunteer organizations, in retail and consulting settings—wherever questions get asked. And too quickly, answered by the asker.

There's nothing wrong with that opening question— "Where would you like to go for dinner, dear?" The trouble is, in our example: The question's asker wasn't listening for an answer, and actually filled in answers instead of listening.

The message: When you ask a question, make it a genuine one. Ask. Stop. Be quiet. Listen for the answer. Look like you're listening closely. It's vital that those of whom you ask questions know you actually care about *their answer* to the question you have posed.

Take an Appreciative Inquiry[12] approach to learning about people. In keeping with the discipline of positive change first articulated by David Cooperider and Suresh Srivastva in 1987, ask people to think of a time when the ideal situation played out.

What happened? How did they get that result? Envisioning the ideal outcome is what allows people to dream and to imagine the best possible way to replicate the ideal. This approach allows all parties to envision and dwell upon the positive and what's working instead of what's wrong and how to fix it. There is a point of view that says: "What we dwell upon grows." I'm choosing to plant positive seeds and water them with thoughts of replicating flowers instead of weeds!

Combine an appreciative approach with a formula developed by Wilson Learning. [13] Using the acronym F·O·R·E, ask people about the following:

Family and friends · How many children do they have? What are their names, genders, interests? (Watch their eyes light up when they talk about them.) Whose companionship do they enjoy the most and why? Large groups or small, intimate ones? What's the greatest experience they can recall sharing with loved ones? Let them talk while you listen.

Occupation · What got them to their current job? What has been the most successful aspect of their career? In detail, why? What do they like about their current job? What excites them? What are they passionate about? What makes their heart sing? What would they attempt to do if they knew they could not fail? What would they change about their job to make it ideal?

Recreation · Are they sports enthusiasts? Do they enjoy chess, reading, going to the theater, opera? Do they enjoy travel? Where, and in what climate? What's the most exciting trip they ever took? With whom? What did they like the most? What are the top ten destinations still left to visit? By when? With whom?

Expectations · What do they want out of life? What are they willing to trade off or delay? Do they have written goals? How far out? What's their big dream, the one with no limits? What are their "21 reasons to succeed" (i.e., things they'll spend their time, money, energy, and creativity to be, have and do)? By now, you'll have picked up on behavioral clues indicating whether the person is introverted or extroverted, analytical or emotion-driven, shy or bold, meticulous or a perfectionist, optimist or pessimist in outlook. In his book *More Than Words*, author Ed Howell labels people variously as lions, porpoises, koalas and foxes, offering strategies for recognizing and responding to these loose "types." [14] You may find his approach useful.

To begin this dialogue, it will be most helpful for you first to have completed for yourself the exercise of discovering your own positive motivators—your own "21 reasons to succeed." Give it a try now and see how quickly you can complete the list. I'll start the list with an item of my own, just to prime the pump…

21 Reasons to Succeed (things I really want in my life):

1.   Fresh flowers in my home and office at all times.
2.   _____
3.   _____
4.   _____
5.   _____
6.   _____
7.   _____
8.   _____
9.   _____
10. _____
11. _____
12. _____
13. _____
14. _____

15. _____

16. _____

17. _____

18. _____

19. _____

20. _____

21. _____

Besides being a great icebreaker for team building, this is a fun activity to use for engaging with family members. Especially with children, whose interests and motivators change as they grow older. Besides, they don't want to be "held in their history" of childhood any more than we do! Revisiting this exercise can be both a thoughtful and playful way to re-engage with members of the family we don't see often.

Ask the right questions. Sometimes asking questions isn't for the purpose of learning how to inspire others to action. Rather, it's simply to gain information or clarity in order to make an informed decision. A couple of years ago I damaged my knee while lifting weights. The resulting injury, torn knee cartilage, had the potential to be career limiting, and was painful enough for me to try a variety of non-traditional approaches before resorting to orthopedic counsel. I did not want to have surgery for a variety of reasons, not the least of which was a planned trip to China and no time for recuperation.

I really liked my doctor and had a lot of confidence in him. He didn't flinch as I asked questions and gave all the reasons I didn't want to have surgery. Finally, I asked, "What would you do if this were your knee?" Much to my surprise, he answered, "When it was my knee, I didn't have time for surgery, either. So I just took anti-inflammatory medicine and let the knee rest, giving it time."

I asked, "Do you mean this can heal itself?"

"No," he replied, "but it can stop hurting enough to get back to normal functioning." That is what I wanted…and be able to exercise, walking at a reasonable pace, so I asked him, "Did you continue to exercise while it was recovering?" and he replied, "Yes, intermittently."

Wow! Asking the right questions was critical. I don't know for sure, but I don't think the doctor would have volunteered that information, had I not been both respectful and persistent. With patience (and acupuncture for the first time in my life), I was able to avoid the dreaded surgery. I have now resumed my previous exercise pace, without weight lifting, and both the orthopedic surgeon and my internist have convinced me that my routine is quite enough for maintaining good health.

Finally, the defining questions can sometimes be posed simply to elicit more information and show interest. Examples:

- How do you mean that?
- Can you tell me more?
- Really – how so?
- Is there anything (else) I should know?

This last kind of question can be particularly effective when you need a quick update to make a rapid decision. It cuts straight to the heart of whatever is most relevant. Ask questions to resolve problems. Jo Lynn Baker, a former Midas franchisee, uses questions to understand another's point of view as a step in resolving problems:

> I am a firm believer in asking questions to help me understand the other person's perspective and open passages that move towards resolution of problems. If I ask a good, open-ended question and then remain quiet and listen, I learn much about the other person and that individual's perspective on the problem. I try not to ask "yes" or "no" questions; they can lead to dead-end conversations. I use questions to start off confrontations that I want to move to resolutions. I give the other person the first opportunity to speak. I will follow up with more questions to draw them into a deeper, more revealing conversation.

This is excellent advice to apply in any relationship, and especially effective for taking a proactive, customer-service approach toward avoiding conflict.

For a thorough resource with exhaustive applications, I recommend *The Question Book* by Bobb Biehl, referencing ninety different experts on every conceivable topic you might encounter. [15]

> *He who asks a question is a fool for five minutes. He who does not ask a question remains a fool forever.*
> — Chinese proverb

Think About It!

Can you think of a situation in your personal life that might be aided by asking the right questions? Make a note of it and plan a strategy for gathering the information you need:

_____

_____

_____

_____

How could asking questions help you better to understand someone with whom you are now attempting to develop a better working relationship? Describe the situation and identify questions you might ask...

_____

_____

_____

_____

You'll find more space to think through these and related questions in Chapter 8—Your Thinking Cap.

chapter 4

Pay Attention!

Applying truth...
> *The deepest principle of human nature is the craving to be appreciated.*
>
> — William James

Once you have people's answers to the questions outlined in Chapter 3, you will have discovered their motivators—that is, what brings them pleasure and where they have already experienced pain that they would like to avoid in the future. You will know what will inspire them to give 100%. You will know how to encourage and uplift them. You will know how to show that you appreciate them. You will have major clues as to what will build the relationship into a true friendship.

Let me give you an example. One of my friends is allergic to chocolate. Sad to say, chocolate makes her sick. It didn't take me long to figure out: don't make my fabulous fudge sauce for dessert when Jackie comes to dinner—it would make her feel like I'm not paying attention!

By noticing how much a vegetarian friend appreciates my attention to detail—not just to the fact she eats vegetables, but to which ones and how she likes them cooked—I have begun asking everyone what their dietary preferences are when planning a dinner party. This way, no one goes away hungry and, better yet, everyone feels that their preferences are really important. "You must eat—so eat *well*," my husband always says.

And it is possible to please everyone invited to any party, if I just ask and pay attention! I've extended this practice of asking about food preferences or allergies before each seminar so the caterer can make provision for special requests (except for one irascible attendee who asked for a steak, medium rare, accompanied by portabella mushrooms!).

An artist friend learned how telling her truth quicker, faster got her what she *really* wanted—more time. She requested that she be removed from distribution lists for forwarded e-mail, regardless of how loving or tempting the message. Further, when taking her new career to the next level, she asked that friends refrain from calling her art studio during business hours. Otherwise, she realized, she'd never meet demanding deadlines for promised work at important art shows. That kind of honesty never offends me!

Be present. Sometimes the best way to pay attention is simply to stop what we're doing and give 100% of ourselves to the person talking. This may mean interrupting a task at hand (or negotiating a more appropriate time by telling our truth quicker, faster). It may mean putting down our newspaper or getting away from the computer, instead of

giving an absentminded response of "Hmm?" or "Uh-huh."
Personally, I find it a bit irritating to have to repeat
information, and I do my best as a seminar leader to ensure
that participants are giving each other undivided attention
when thoughts, observations or feelings are being shared. I
also request that cell phones and pagers be turned off or set
to vibrate for the same reason.

Sometimes, I find it necessary to just stop talking until
others are silent or—with a family member or intimate
friend—actually cradle their face in my hands, gently and
lovingly, and say, "I really need you to pay attention to what
I am about to say." It's almost as effective to lean forward and
place my hand on their forearm and make the request. I'm
not suggesting, however, that you do this with a stranger or
business colleague unless you have permission!

Listen and respond with empathy[16]. Some parts of
life are set up for winners and losers—the game of chess
comes to mind immediately, as do many team sports. In
relationships, however, I knew intuitively that each person
could be a winner, if we agreed to play by rules which
encourage and reward behavior that finds a winning
solution for all the players.

Paying attention is necessary in order to listen and
respond with empathy. I discovered that empathetic
listening helps me learn another's truth and ensure that the
meaning is clearly understood by all parties. It leads to the

process of designing mutual, win-win solutions. Even when everyone doesn't agree, we can be agreeable for the sake of winning the relationship game! Nothing is gained when two people defend their own point of view and don't attempt to walk in the other person's shoes.

Returning to Jo Lynn Baker for more advice, she shared a relevant story that demonstrates perfectly the IBC win-win:

> As an employer of 35 people, I am often called upon to resolve conflicts with employees. One of my employees was disgruntled when he did not receive his full week's pay for a week he was absent from work due to a personal situation. He did not have any vacation pay available to cover the week. Although he was not at work full-time that week, he did work two half-days and checked in with the shop by telephone daily.
>
> Our personnel clerk was under the impression that he was absent all week, and did not pay him at all for the week. He was very upset and felt cheated and unappreciated. I called him and said, "I understand you have concerns about your paycheck. Tell me how you're feeling."
>
> He told me when he had checked in by phone and what hours he had come into the shop. He also explained that he felt he gave a lot of himself to his

job, often working many extra hours just to ensure his shop was running smoothly. He felt the company should have paid him for that week because he was a good, devoted employee.

I asked him for clarification. "Do you feel you are entitled to a full week's pay for working two half-days and for calling in by telephone the other days?"

He sheepishly answered "no."

I asked a deeper question that would help me understand his thought process further. "Let's say this same situation happened with one of your subordinates — your helper worked the same schedule you just described. How would you handle it?"

"Well, I wouldn't give him his full pay, but I would give him something," he answered.

I closed in for details. "And what would that be?" I asked. He gave his recommendation as to how he would pay the employee.

Then I moved toward resolution. "So, do you feel that same formula would be fair and appropriate in your situation?"

We were now well on our way to a final agreement.

When I first called him, he was angry and hurt, and his emotions were escalating. When he'd had a chance to share his feelings and thoughts, the anger dissipated *and he was able to reason with me and see a fair solution. When he looked at the situation from my perspective by placing himself in the boss's shoes, he saw that his expectation of full pay for part-time hours was unrealistic, and I was able to understand his view and recognize an oversight our personnel department had made.*

Asking questions is key to opening a discussion and allowing for an honest exchange of ideas and feelings. Customers, employees and friends need to be able to talk about their feelings, their experiences and their expectations. Sometimes, just being able to talk about their concerns helps them feel better even without the expected results. Asking questions shows the other person that you are interested in their problem and you desire to know more.

Paying attention is good business. "Business goes where it's invited and stays where it is welcome." I don't know who said that, but I certainly do believe it to be true, whether it's an internal customer or an external customer. Anyone in sales has been taught to pick up clues about people from pictures, plaques and awards in their office. In the Western culture, we know that eye contact, a firm handshake and remembering a person's name are habits that can you win more business.

I make notes (and yes, sometimes I have to pull away

from networking for a minute to capture them on the back of a new acquaintance's business card). With that assisted memory, I can do my best to reward, recognize, and appreciate people in the ways most meaningful to them. I call it "The Platinum Rule"—do unto others the way they want to be "done unto." You will be amazed at the way people respond!

Regardless of how sincere, respectful, and skilled we are as communicators, we will be all be faced with difficult conversations. For those of us who avoid confrontation at all costs, the result can be time consuming and emotionally draining. To be effective leaders in all areas of life, we must learn to effectively and efficiently deal in this area of difficulty. The best advice I learned from a psychologist friend was: "Never back someone in a corner. Give them the opportunity to save face." Equally, take responsibility and prepare for sticky conversations, so you won't be blindsided.

The IBC way might look like this, as between a hypothetical Brad and a not-so-hypothetical Shelley...

> "Shelley," Brad asks, "I'd like to sit down for about half an hour to discuss a project we're working on. Can we do that now?"
>
> "Brad, give me fifteen minutes. What's the specific topic? What do I need to do in order to be ready for you?"

"It's the leadership training workbook for ABC Industries, Shelley, and I'm stuck on developing appropriate scenario examples for the learners' role-plays."

"Great. I'll finish here, grab the file, and find you in fifteen. Conference room H okay? We'll hear each other out, then brainstorm some ideas. I'm confident we can meet the deadline."

One final, important consideration about empathetic listening and paying attention: how do you respond to fear...your own fear, or someone else's fear? How do you draw it out when you sense it, knowing that it may be paralyzing you...or someone you know? Instead of avoiding fear and hoping it will go away, here's a way to bring way to bring closure to decision-making that appears to be bogged down by fear. It's my new favorite question to ask when myself when feeling fear about a decision, suggested by Mary Jo Asmus' in her blog post, "A Question of Courage"

Is it the right thing to do? [17]

If the answer to the question is a resounding *yes*, I resolve to trust myself, face my fear, and move ahead. I also resolve to ask that courage question when my teammates, family, and friends seek my counsel. The question...and answer...can apply equally well to a personal or professional dilemma.

Go to your bosom: knock there,
and ask your heart what it doth know.

— William Shakespeare

Think About It!

Tom Hopkins, one of the greatest salesmen of all time, says this:

> Because I understood that building relationships is what selling is all about, I began early in my career to send thank you notes to people. I set a daily goal to send ten thank you notes, which meant that I had to meet and get the names of at least ten people every day. I sent thank you notes to people I met briefly, people I showed properties to, people I talked with on the telephone, and people I actually helped to own new homes. I became a thank you note-writing fool!
>
> And guess what happened? By the end of my third year in sales, my business was 98% referrals. The people I had expressed gratitude to were happy to send me new clients as a reward for making them feel appreciated and important. [18]

To whom should you send thank-you notes this week?

_____

_____

_____

_____

Beyond notes of congratulations, do you call to express your interest when your hear news about people you know? Do you ever send an email congratulating someone? Do you often send a copy of an article, website URL, or a book reference which might interest a friend or colleague? What more could you do along these lines?

_____

_____

_____

_____

_____

Think of a time when you learned something meaningful or important about someone. Did you take time to really listen as an ally? Did you withhold your personal judgments, criticism or advice? Did you make sure you understood the meaning _behind_ the words? The question behind the question? [19]

_____

_____

_____

How can you apply this "Pay Attention" behavior to improve one particular relationship _today_?

Person: _____

Situation or occasion: _____
_____

Action you'll take: _____
_____

By when: _____

Bob Burg, author of *Endless Referrals*, says…"People do business with, and refer business to, people they know, like and trust." [20] By first paying attention to what's important to people…acknowledging their wins…showing that we care about their success…asking how we can help them, specifically…we continue to build relationships with them, authentically. And perhaps they will reciprocate (though that is not the point.)

_____
_____
_____
_____
_____

What else do you think might make a difference in you being more successful in your business or personal life?

_____
_____
_____

Here's an especially tough question, demanding some personal honesty: What are you pretending not to know?

_____

_____

_____

_____

Finally, when all else fails to resolve an especially sticky situation, ask yourself, "Is this a ditch I want to die in?" If the answer is _no_, find a way to diffuse the situation, without blaming. Perhaps paying attention means re-engaging with your truth at a deeper level. "Your friendship is more important than our disagreement" will totally change the energy of your exchange. Or simply, "Can we just agree to disagree, respectfully?"

You'll find more space to think through these and related questions in Chapter 8—Your Thinking Cap.

chapter **5**

Keep Your Agreements

Accepting truth…
> *'I am responsible' is the most powerful affirmation*
> *a person can say.*
>
> — Brian Tracy

Fifth Axiom: Most of us make and keep agreements less well than we believe. Often, for many of us, when things go awry, it's "someone else's fault." It's the other guy. Not me. I held up my end—but those people… Often, however, it's we ourselves who are to blame—at least in part.

But blame isn't the point. Blame is about the past. As we see from Brian Tracy's famous remark, the real point is about the future, and what we can do now to make that future better. The real point is: Let's take responsibility for the agreements we make, and for keeping them.

Sometimes, the issue is failing to keep an agreement we've made. We "forget." We "get busy." Sometimes, the problem is the agreement itself. A common problem: an agreement that isn't specific enough, isn't well expressed. Witness the business meeting whose members resolve to "take the necessary action" to rectify an issue or take advantage of an opportunity. Weeks go by. And, because the group never said, specifically, what "the necessary action" was, nobody does anything.

Keep your agreements. In its purest form, this behavior is about personal mastery and self-discipline. We cannot begin to lead others with integrity until we have learned to lead ourselves effectively and consistently. Taking personal responsibility means growing up and doing what you say you will do so that people think of you as a person who is dependable. What you say will be done, simply because you say so. My earliest conscious recollection comes from Dr. Seuss's *Horton Hatches the Egg*: "I meant what I said, and I said what I meant; an elephant's faithful 100%." [21]

I'll bet you know people who are perpetually late. Whether for a dinner date or a business meeting, they know very well what the starting time is, but they still arrive late. Maybe you've even played the game, "We'll just tell him dinner is thirty minutes earlier so we won't be kept waiting to eat."

As much as I hate to admit it, I used to have the habit of *always* showing up late. People would be waiting for me, and I never thought about what kind of message my behavior was sending—though I certainly got irritated when *I* had to wait for anyone! Somewhere along the way, it dawned upon me how selfish and arrogant this bad habit made me appear.

Even though I didn't consciously mean to, I was

sending a message that I was more important and my time more valuable than anyone else's. I was horrified, and vowed I'd break the habit.

Now, I'm even more aghast, realizing the amount of time, energy, creativity and money wasted, while others waited for my appearance. Can you think of a time when you experience that happening, even today? Can you envision a practical intervention?

Re-negotiate your agreements. In reality, there were times when I realized that I could not keep an agreement, long before the deadline. I analyzed and agonized — sometimes procrastinated, with painful results. Finally, I found the key to building and maintaining the healthy relationships which are so vital to my happiness was to respect others' time and needs — to the same degree that I want mine respected.

For me, this means re-negotiating an agreement as soon as I realize it is necessary. Even if it's a weekend, when a family emergency has arisen. When my father died late on a Sunday night, I called my client, knowing that my assigned training for the following weekend needed to be covered. She was both surprised and appreciative. The last-minute, higher-priced airplane ticket for my replacement trainer was never mentioned.

On a more regular basis, striving to be 100% responsible about timeliness, I exchange cell phone numbers with everyone involved in a meeting... just in case the unexpected happens. And I keep my cell phone turned on until everyone arrives. That way, anyone who needs to re-negotiate can do so when confronted with a traffic jam or other delay.

No matter what the situation, honoring agreements consistently earns higher levels of trust, respect and credibility. Today if I'm late for a meeting, people say, "Something must have happened, or we would have heard from Shelley by now." Usually, it's just my Smart Alec phone acting up!

I am responsible for myself, regardless. Knowing that sometimes things do go awry, I take along reading material, thank-you notes to write, or a project in progress. That way, if I'm meeting with someone who runs late I always have something productive to do, instead of getting impatient while waiting. It makes for a much more pleasant meeting when I take responsibility for my own frame of mind, regardless of the circumstances!

I love this story told by Brian Tracy, in *The Phoenix Seminar for Maximum Achievement*.[22] He tells of numerous people with relationship problems who have complained about how unhappy they are, how they don't love one another, and how they are generally miserable. He listens empathetically and then asks, "What are you going to do about it?"

Some simply play the victim role and answer, "Well, there's nothing I *can* do about it."

Brian will ask the person how old they are, subtract this figure from their current life expectancy, and say, "Do you plan to stay in this unhappy, miserable relationship for another thirty-five years?"

In all honesty, he says, the answer must be *No*.

Brian Tracy is certainly not advocating divorce by this response. What he is advocating personal responsibility. No matter how badly we mess up, no matter what mistake we make, the redemption is found in what we do to correct the mistake and move on with our lives.

You never find yourself until you face the truth.
— Pearl Bailey

Think About It!

Today, what area of your life needs the affirmation *I am responsible*? Is it a relationship, your job, your boss? Describe the situation and circumstances…

_____

_____

_____

_____

_____

_____

By taking personal responsibility for your part in the situation, how do you visualize the outcome moving nearer your ideal?

_____

_____

_____

_____

_____

You'll find more space to think through these and related questions in Chapter 8—Your Thinking Cap.

chapter **6**

Give and Receive Accountability

Living your truth…
> *The measure of a man's character is what he would do*
> *if he knew he would never be found out.*
> — Thomas B. Macaulay

The distinction between being *responsible* and being *accountable*. I'm often asked in seminars for the difference between behaviors 5 and 6 of the Integrity-Based Communications method.

Quite simply, being *responsible* means that I do what I say I will do.

Being *accountable* means that I don't make excuses for the decisions or mistakes *I* make, blaming other people or circumstances. Too often, we indulge excuses for the purpose of allowing ourselves to slide into the "wasn't-my-fault" zone. Why? Because most of us hate taking blame. Yes, there are figurative or literal bullets which might strike us, buses which might run us over, freeing us from blame. But this discussion isn't about blame. No, blame is a matter of negative moral judgment—usually made by others, sometimes by dark, unkindly corners within ourselves—and blame simply isn't in issue here. What is at issue is choice.

If I'm late for our appointment this afternoon, it's because I chose to take this route rather than that, chose to answer "just one more" email, or chose to take a phone call, rather than let it go to voice mail, as I was walking out the door.

In every case, it is I who make the choices about my actions, and I must hold myself accountable for the outcomes. Such outcomes can be immediate—the "one more email" I chose to answer meant I couldn't get there by two o'clock. Outcomes can also be more distant, more indirect. Even the proverbial flat tire most of us have used at least once as an excuse is, often as not, the result of haste in driving or of our decision two months ago not to buy that new tire we knew we needed.

Sometimes, taking responsibility is a very hard thing to do, because it's easier to fall back into the irresponsible "victim" role and blame some person or some external circumstance, whether that circumstance be the rain on the road, the week's workload, an ex-spouse's anger or abuse, even childhood hurts.

Carol Waugh, Independent Executive National Vice President with Arbonne International, gives a classic setback-to-comeback example. This is her personal story about the role of accountability in successful leadership...

> *I found out the hard way that it takes courage to be accountable for one's actions! As the leader of a*

*huge marketing group of "wanna-be"
entrepreneurs, being accountable for my own
actions and success led me toward personal
development in my interaction with others. Being a
strong personality, not everyone wanted to hear my
truth quicker, faster. As I worked through the jungle
of personalities, I began to understand that there are
many truths with different slants. I looked in the
mirror with great interest as to how I could be a
better person with the highest standard of integrity
based on my values and principles. There are
different styles of personalities that can work in
win-win relationships if some basic principles are
followed.*

*The principle I've wanted to follow is the Golden
Rule: "Do unto others as you would have them do to
you." What a simple truth that gets bent with our
own inadequacies! Our reality is that we mess up
sometimes.*

*Most of us "blame" and do not acknowledge our
part in the situation. A leader, however, is willing to
take responsibility for a decision that is a mistake
and willing to be held accountable.*

*At one point in my career I made a "political
mistake," and as a result, I faced a "fight or flight"
situation. When I decided to fight my way back from*

*humiliation and damage to my reputation, I began
with a sincere apology for those who felt wronged.
What I learned was that when there was a
misunderstanding and misinterpretation of the
facts, my reputation suffered and all the good I had
done for years was forgotten. Apologizing for my
part in what went wrong led me to a positive-
thinking faith that gave me confidence in my own
abilities. I had to become willing to be accountable
for my mistakes, my actions, my failures, and my
successes. Criticism — or feedback — should inspire
me to better. It was a tough lesson to learn.*

   *It's hard to find people who are brave enough to
accept responsibility. The fear of being held liable for
mistakes is enough to frighten many of us from
leadership. I chose to embrace personal
responsibility and accept the challenges of
leadership, thereby reaping the benefits of personal
growth and enjoying financial freedom for my
family because I had developed the courage to be
accountable.*

When I'm successfully being accountable, I'm *living in
integrity.* There have been times in my life when I've lived
out of integrity, however, and deeply disappointed both
myself …and others. I've also learned that living out of
integrity has its own peculiar blend of stresses. In the midst

of marital problems some years and a lifetime ago, which deteriorated into divorce, I was embezzled by a "best friend" and double-crossed by a business partner who defaulted on rent. My response at the time: I heard what I wanted to hear and justified the rest, while my financial common sense was faltering. I ignored my "sixth sense" and judged myself wrong for not trusting these people—even when all the evidence showed I definitely shouldn't trust them!

During this time, while I was living out of integrity, I borrowed money and didn't keep my agreements about timely repayment, despite good intentions. I also asked people to do things *they* didn't want to do because *I* didn't want to do what needed to be done. At the same time, I no longer enjoyed my work. I felt that I wasn't making a meaningful contribution, wasn't behaving as a responsible steward. Lacking passion for my work, I felt I was selling out, even though I was on my own and knew that I had to support myself. My self-respect was ebbing, lower than ever, and I knew I had to change my life. I felt as if I were dying inside. As I look back, now that I understand what I can do about stress, I believe I was indeed, in a powerful sense, dying. Certainly my moral life was in mortal danger.

Sixth Axiom: We are all afraid of accountability. I'll hold this axiom is dead true, for everyone—except for a *tiny* percentage of people who do not care anything about what anyone, anywhere thinks of them. These people we call sociopaths. For the rest of us, it matters what people think of us—friends, family, colleagues, employers, and those we associate with in educational, social, recreational and volunteer settings.

Being individuals, we're afraid in different degrees— some a little, or only occasionally, others a great deal. Being individuals, we are afraid of different things, of different parts or aspects of the accountability process.

Some are afraid of disappointing others. Consider the woman who's promised her boss a certain document by Thursday noon. She hasn't got it done. Indeed, yesterday, Wednesday, she knew it couldn't get done in time. But rather than call and negotiate a new deadline, she simply, as it were, "closed her eyes real tight" and hoped he wouldn't notice that the document didn't arrive until Friday.

Others are afraid of their own guilt. We all know the feeling: "Oh, here I go—late for the meeting again!" For some, the fear is of guilt's close cousin—embarrassment. If you've been, or you've ever encountered, a person who often won't ask for clarification, ask for a repeat of instructions or an explanation, or ask *how* to do an instructed task, a certain fear of embarrassment may be the cause. The issue may be fear of looking silly, looking "dumb," or looking as if you haven't been listening.

Some of us are afraid of others' reactions, and those

reactions, in turn, become the trigger or rationale for lots of behavior in us. The boss who yells creates employees who are afraid to do *anything*, let alone disobey. If you've ever felt yourself cowering inside, it may be in fear of someone else's reaction.

Many people are afraid of being wrong, or of having this known. "Being right"—knowing the right answer—is a vital driver for many among us. For these, being mistaken about some truth or issue is itself a fear, because the very idea of "being wrong" would threaten their sense of identity. No matter whether the issue is as big as finding the right economic strategy for a giant corporation or a nation, or as trite as the winning word in tonight's Scrabble ™ game: The prospect of "being wrong" haunts some of us. It is, overwhelmingly, fear which we let prevent us from becoming, and remaining, truly accountable.

Overcoming that fear takes effort and, often, outright courage. As I struggled with my own growth toward a fuller and better personal accountability, I remembered some of my earliest personal development work, The Dale Carnegie Course,[23] which I took to help me overcome my fear of public speaking. What had stuck with me was the advice never to accept a speaking engagement for a topic on which I'd not earned the right to speak. Rather than saying "no" outright, however, I could re-negotiate the topic and commit to speaking about an area of expertise where I had both demonstrated competence *and* personal interest.

For some reason, I remembered that advice and realized that I had to renegotiate my life and what it was all about. I had come to believe that the work I was doing was a reflection of what my inner life was—empty. Gradually, I realized that I was the problem, not my circumstances. In other words, I was becoming accountable. I considered that maybe my very thinking had gotten me into my current situation and getting out had to begin with changing my mind. I don't remember who actually said it first, but I do believe it is true: "Change your thoughts and you change your life."

I felt hopeful as I considered making a career change. I wanted to experience a sense of purpose and authenticity, doing something I believed positive and worthwhile. A prayer I saw—"Lord, reform thy world, beginning with me"—became my daily petition.

By coincidence—I believed rather more in coincidence back then—I was asked to speak under the rubric "Living a Balanced Life,"(now part of my *Living on Purpose* seminar[24]). In my talk, I admitted that I was focusing my attention on living a balanced life. I was honest about my shortcomings and the steps I was taking to become more balanced. Amazingly, I found that audiences actually *liked* my vulnerability and authenticity. I wasn't whining and I wasn't preaching; I was simply telling my story. As bad as things were for me at times, people found hope in my message because I was being accountable, moving ahead and expressing good humor about the mistakes I had made.

My mistakes of the past are what I now term "high growth learning opportunities." I was simply enrolled in the school of continuing education—not the school of hard knocks! I found it easier to laugh as I discovered people were laughing with me, not at me.

As I began to live, striving to be as truthful as I could be—every day, in every situation—I became less embarrassed and more empowered. I literally reclaimed the personal power I had lost along the way when I lost myself. It seemed that every time I took a risk, whether the outcome was exactly what I wanted or not, I was able to feel better about myself just because I had stepped outside of my comfort zone to improve myself.

By now, I had taken all three courses of the Life Design Seminars and had come to believe that the ideal career for me might be the personal development path I had been pursuing. Soon thereafter, I attended Brian Tracy's *The Phoenix Seminar for Maximum Achievement*,[25] and there I felt "the right connection." I became a serious student of, then a facilitator for that seminar, and continued to sharpen my saw with Stephen Covey, Wayne Dyer, Deepak Chopra, Marianne Williamson, Zig Ziglar, John Maxwell and others. I began to spend more time with purpose-driven people, and less time tolerating people still wallowing in negativity and self-pity. I learned how I could choose either to distance myself from such people or to turn negative conversations into positive ones—without making people wrong or even pointing out what I was doing. I was learning to discern what was my business, and what was not. I started asking for permission before giving my opinion. I grew a sense of inner peace, even though life wasn't perfect, by any stretch.

Then I met Bonnie Taylor, an amazing person who facilitated a life-changing seminar I attended, Nikken's *Humans Being More.* [26] A woman of wonderful spirit and heart, Bonnie's life purpose is to experience joy by giving it away—and she does it impeccably. She became my champion as I pursued becoming a facilitator for *Humans Being More* and, later, a leadership development facilitator for Nikken University.

At this stage I began to understand more robustly about alignment of purpose, values and beliefs, and actual behavior. No question, *Humans Being More* allowed me to tap into what I didn't know about myself and how I was blocking myself from my highest good. This was when I realized how I was keeping myself from attracting the life partner I really wanted.

Two months later, I met John Baur. When we married, I realized my heart's desire was to spend more time at home, to give up my workaholic ways. My life circumstances had changed, along with accompanying values about home and a spiritual relationship with a committed life partner.

By learning to recognize that truth, I'm freed now to do work that truly makes my heart sing, which work includes facilitating my seminar, *Living on Purpose: Tools for Building the Life You Really Want.* [27] Over the seminar's two days, I'm able to share the truths that helped me to unlock my own potential and liberate myself from the ways I was holding myself back, to connect with my own purpose and life mission, and to become the person that would attract the perfect husband for me (which is why I adore having couples in my classes, to this very day).

Galileo once said, "You cannot teach people anything. You can only help them discover it within themselves." *That's* what a good facilitator does…and intentionally models that behavior for others to follow.

Now, on those occasions when I do slip into old habits and blame other people or circumstances for my lack of delivering what I promise, I notice very quickly that I am playing victim. I become more confident and courageous as I "walk my talk" and am consistently accountable for the results and outcomes in my life. This is what I call "giving up the blame game, moving from victim to victor." The first five IBC behaviors are ineffectual—they add up to nothing—if I refuse to be accountable for my choices and my actions.

I also find myself enjoying higher levels of energy

and good health. Quite authentically, I radiate happiness and joy. Those rare times when I realize I'm not in a positive frame of mind, I can make a choice to change that reality. Simply by changing my mind, the new, replacement thought will knock out the old one and I can begin again, taking the high road.

Try to live your life so that you wouldn't be afraid to sell the family parrot to the town gossip.
— Will Rogers

Think About It!

Whom or what have you blamed today for something that's not working in your life? Your boss, spouse, business associate, the economy, politics? Describe the situation…

_____

_____

_____

_____

What would be your ideal outcome for this situation?

_____

_____

_____

_____

What self-intervention could you perform to get what you really want from the situation?

_____

_____

_____

You'll find more space to think through these and related questions in Chapter 8—Your Thinking Cap.

chapter 7

Living on Purpose

Using your truth…

> *It takes courage to grow up and be who we really are.*

— e. e. cummings

Integrity-Based Communications (IBC):

1. Tell your truth quicker, faster.
2. Ask for what you want.
3. Ask questions to discover others' motivators.
4. Pay attention!
5. Keep your agreements.
6. Give and receive accountability.

I have been using IBC for many years, in my quest for self-knowledge and continuing improvement. By becoming aware of my values and what those mean to me in each relationship or circumstance, I am able to make choices, consistent with whom I know myself to be today. This is how I stay on purpose and model integrity.

I take to heart what Albert Schweitzer said: "Example is not the main thing in influencing others. It's the only thing."

Or, as Ralph Waldo Emerson put it, "What you do speaks so loudly that I cannot hear what you say."

Stated simply, integrity is "walking the talk." It's consistently aligning your attitude, your words, your tone of voice, your nonverbal communications, and your daily actions with your values and beliefs. Here's an example from my own life...

One of my values is to respect every human being. My underlying belief is that I can learn from every person I meet. These were put to the test one day when I went to the grocery store with one of my girlfriends, her eight year-old son and his friend. While the two boys clowned around in the store, one broke a big jar of pickles in the middle of an aisle. In that moment, I was able to choose to live in integrity, for which I'm grateful. Rather than becoming impatient or angry and making him wrong, I was able to see this as a learning experience and respect his right to make mistakes. Together, we found the store manager, helped clean up the mess, and the boy learned that one doesn't leave pickles, broken glass, and juice on the floor to cause problems for others. It became a memorable lesson for this youngster in telling the truth ("I did it."), taking responsibility ("I was running, hit the jar and broke it.") and being accountable ("I'll help clean up the mess I made.").

Would I dare to say that I demonstrate this degree of levelheadedness and maturity all the time? Sadly, no. But I do try to recognize when I fall short and determine how I could have done it better, how I might handle the situation differently next time. Of these two, it's the future I try to focus on — the next time rather than the last time. The major trouble with advice in the form of "could have" and "should have," even when you're advising yourself, is that it's advice you can't follow: The past is broken, and it is beyond fixing. "Could have" advice, by itself, is useless at best, and at worst can lead us back in to the land of blame and endless guilt. But let the "could have" transform into "next time I will..." and you'll have placed past and future in their proper perspective.

When I realize I'm off course, I make a correction—in that very moment if I possibly can—and communicate my "new truth" in whatever manner feels most appropriate. By my learning to do so, my life has become more than ever before filled with positive outcomes, rewarding results, and nurturing experiences.

Tell me, I forget. Show me, I remember. Involve me, I learn and make it my own. I recognize the truth of this Chinese proverb, and so the next step is yours. I encourage you to incorporate the six behaviors of IBC into your life— *daily*. Perform the chapter-end exercises for yourself. Very soon you will see—as many people have—that using truth really *can* attract your heart's desires to you.

Sincerely, I'd really like to hear your success stories. When you're ready, please e-mail me at shelley@shelleybaur.com.

To give real service you must add something which cannot be bought or measured with money, and that is sincerity and integrity.

— Donald A. Adams

chapter 8

Your Thinking Cap

This chapter 8 is *yours*. It's a place for you to think through more thoroughly all of the questions posed at the ends of the six chapters on the six behaviors of Integrity-Based Communications (IBC).

Write. Mark up this part of the book. Make it your own. In fact, you'll be capping off your IBC learning experience only if you make use, beyond merely thinking, of this opportunity to write about what you've learned, what you plan to do toward a new you.

Each of the six behaviors of Integrity-Based Communications has its own section within this chapter.

Tell Your Truth Quicker, Faster

Think of two occasions…one that occurred weeks, months, even years ago…one that's occurred within recent days or a couple of weeks …when you didn't tell your truth quicker, faster…

Today's date: ———————————————————

Situation #1…Long ago…
When did the situation occur? What's the truth you now

Tell Your Truth Quicker, Faster continued

wish you'd told quicker, faster? What happened in the
result?

_____

_____

_____

_____

Is there anything you might say or do now, even at this late
date, to better the situation by telling your truth? If not, then
how will you, when a situation like this arises again, tell
your truth quicker, faster?

_____

_____

_____

_____

_____

Situation #2...Recent days or weeks...

When did this more recent situation occur? What's the truth
you now wish you'd told quicker, faster? What happened in
the result?

_____

_____

_____

_____

Tell Your Truth Quicker, Faster continued

_____

_____

What could you say or do now to better the situation by telling your truth? If nothing, then how will you, when a situation like this arises again, tell your truth quicker, faster?

_____

_____

_____

_____

_____

_____

_____

_____

_____

_____

Ask for What You Want

What do you *really* want in your future? Try answer in the question using the following open-ended prompts...

> I want work in which I am free to...

> I want a relationship that brings me...

> I want friends with whom I can...

> I want living circumstances that let me...

Ask for What You Want continued

Describe a time you didn't "ask for what you wanted," and what happened in the result...

Describe a time you didn't "ask for what you wanted," and what happened as a result...

Think about a business relationship you're which you could improve by taking a risk and asking for what you want... What will you do?   By when?

Think about a personal relationship you're which you could improve by taking a risk and asking for what you want...What will you do? By when?

Ask Questions to Discover Others' Motivators

Can you think of a situation in your personal life that might be aided by asking the right questions? Make a note of it and plan a strategy for gathering the information you need:

_____

_____

_____

_____

Can you think of a situation in your business life that might be aided by asking the right questions? Make a note of it and plan a strategy for gathering the information you need:

_____

_____

_____

_____

How could asking questions help you better to understand someone with whom you are now attempting to develop a better working relationship? Describe the situation and identify questions you might ask…

_____

_____

_____

_____

Pay Attention

Describe a person to whom you need to pay more or better attention. What, specifically, will you do in order to pay better attention? Specifically, what will you do to show you are paying better attention?

Identify three or more situations—including at least two professional or business situations and one personal or volunteer situation in which you'll resolve to use note-taking both to help you pay attention and to *show* that you're paying attention.

Keep Your Agreements
Give and Receive Accountability

As you look at your life—both business and personal aspects—can you see any general pattern as to accountability? Are there specific people with whom you have or have not been successful at giving and receiving accountability?

Describe a situation in your business life where you need to take responsibility, using the affirmation "I am responsible"…

Describe a situation in your personal life where you need to take responsibility, using the affirmation "I am responsible"...

What new actions will you take today or this week to improve your reputation for accountability? Try for three.

1.

2.

3.

Resources

1. James M. Kouzes and Barry Z. Posner, *Credibility*. New York: Jossey-Bass

2. Juanell Teague. www.JuanellTeague.com

3. Albert Mehrabian. www.businessballs.com/mehrabiancommunications.htm

4. "Key Principles." www.ddiworld.com

5. "Values Clarification." www.integritybasedcommunications.com/greatest-joys-greatest-fears/

6. *Living on Purpose: Tools for Building the Life You Really Want*. www.shelleybaur.com

7. Business Network International. www.bni.com

8. Tim McGuire wrote a syndicated column, "More Than Work" for United Media until 2006. He blogs now at http://cronkite.asu.edu/mcguireblog/

9. Ivan R. Misner, *Givers Gain: The BNI Story*. Upland, California: Paradigm Publishing, 2004.

10. Lewis Carroll, *Through The Looking Glass And What Alice Found There*. London: McMillan and Co., 1872.

11. Stephen R. Covey, *The Seven Habits of Highly Effective People.* New York: Simon & Schuster, 1989.

12. "Appreciative Inquiry." www.appreciativeinquiry.com. See also Diana Whitney and Amanda Trosten-Bloom, *The Power of Appreciative Inquiry: A Practical Guide to Positive Change.* San Francisco: Berrett-Koehler, 2003.

13. Wilson Learning, www.wilsonlearning.com

14. Edward Horrell, *More Than Words.* Memphis: Center for Spoken Communication, Inc., 1995.

15. Bobb Biehl, *The Question Book.* Nashville: Thomas Nelson, Inc., 1993.

16. "Key Principles." www.ddiworld.com

17. Mary Jo Asmus. www,aspire-cs.com/a-question-of-courage

18. Tom Hopkins, www.TomHopkins.com

19. John G. Miller, *QBQ! The Question Behind the Question: Practicing Personal Accountability at Work and in Life.* Putnam Adult, September 9, 2004.

20. Bob Burg, *Endless Referrals.* McGraw-Hill Companies, 1994.

21. Dr. Seuss [pseud.]. *Horton Hatches the Egg.* New York: Random House, 1940.

22. Brian Tracy, *The Phoenix Seminar for Maximum Achievement.* www.tracyint.com/index.php.89.html

23. The Dale Carnegie Course. www.DaleCarnegie.com

24. "Living on Purpose." www.integritybasedcommunications.com/living-on-purpose/

25. Brian Tracy, *The Phoenix Seminar for Maximum Achievement.* http://www.tracyint.com/index.php.89.html

26. *Humans Being More.* Nikken University. www.nikkenu.com

27. *Living on Purpose: Tools for Building the Life You Really Want.* www.shelleybaur.com

About the Author

Shelley Baur's career comprises independent… and corporate business experience in marketing, field sales, communications, training, learning and development. Inspiring people to live on purpose and realize their potential, she has designed materials and conducted workshops for all levels of employees with an emphasis on personal analysis and skill development.

An entrepreneur since 1986, Shelley includes among her clients include Fortune 500 business units, non-profit universities, medical facilities, professional associations and small business owners across North America.

Believing that success depends upon the core value of integrity, Shelley works with people who want to communicate more confidently and work together more authentically and profitably, both face-to-face and online. She serves as a consultant and communication coach to small business owners and professionals in education and business. Seminars she has developed include *Integrity-Based Communications* and *Living on Purpose: Tools for Building the Life You Really Want.* Programs specifically designed for entrepreneurs who are building sales organizations include interviewing, recruiting and hiring, negotiating, consultative selling techniques, team-building and leadership skills, among other topics. Previously Shelley was Vice President of Communications for one of the largest security companies in the U.S.

Shelley is a founding member/past president of the National Association of Women Business Owners (NAWBO) Memphis Chapter, and past president of Sales & Marketing Executives of Memphis. She is an active graduate of Leadership Memphis, and continues her connection with the Society for Human Resource Management, the American Society for Training & Development, Toastmasters International, BNI: Business Network International, Business Over Coffee International, and the University of Memphis, where she mentors and coaches students about life and leadership choices.

What's Next For You?

Where to from here? Depending on where you've begun with the Integrity-Based Communications system—book, keynote speech, workshop or seminar, corporate training, communications coaching, or just a presentation handout—you may want to learn more for your own personal development journey. Or perhaps to take steps for personally managing your own message… and your own career progress.

Shelley and her One Source Associates team have developed, customized, and delivered half-day to one-week learning experiences for all levels of employees, beginning with the core module, Integrity-Based Communications. These include:

- Building Relationships With Integrity-Based Communications

- Building Business Relationships With Integrity-Based Communications

- Building *Better* Business Relationships With Integrity-Based Communications

- Delivering Impactful Messages With Integrity-Based Communications

- Giving and Receiving Effective Feedback With Integrity-Based Communications

- Communicating Across the Generations: Making Meaning For Today's Work Teams

- Practical Applications for Ethical Decision-Making

- Exploring the Ethics of Stewardship and Sustainability

- Truth, Trust and Sustainability

- Integrity-Based Sustainability...From The CEO Through Supply Chain

- Supervisory and Management: Skills and Leadership

- Global Diversity and Inclusion

- Integrity-Based Inclusion...It's More Than Diversity

We're constantly refining and developing new Integrity-Based Communications programs. Please check regularly, sign up for our newsletter, read and comment on our blog, www.integritybasedcommunications.com.

For more information on upcoming public seminars, including, "Living on Purpose: Tools to Build the Life You *Really* Want" go to www.shelleybaur.com or contact shelley@shelleybaur.com.

For options to connect with Shelley at conferences and/or workshop, check her current schedule of activities at www.shelleybaur.com.

Your can find Shelley on LinkedIn, Facebook and Twitter @shelleybaur...
Whichever method of connecting you choose, Shelley invites you to stay in touch. In fact, she really adores hand-written notes, too!

> One Source Associates
> 8312 Wesley Woods Circle
> Memphis, Tennessee 38018-8234
> Email: shelley@shelleybaur.com